What To Expect From Your Property Manager

A Guide for Co-op, Condo and HOA Boards

By Leslie Kaminoff

Published by Highpoint Ventures
144 Crispell Road
Olivebridge, New York 12461
(845) 657-6453

This publication is designed to provide accurate and authoritative information in regard to the subject matter covered. It is distributed with the understanding that the publisher is not engaged in rendering legal, accounting or other professional services. If legal advice or other expert assistance is required, the services of a competent professional person should be sought.

First Edition, First Printing
Printed in Canada
Library of Congress Control Number: 2005920671
ISBN: 0-9764229-0-5

TABLE OF CONTENTS

Dedication

This book is dedicated to my wife Kim and my children, Alexis, Ashley and Justin, whose patience and understanding have supported me through the many long hours, emergency calls and business trips that constantly demand my time as a property manager and CEO. And to the spouses and children of all the professionals in the management industry who put their own lives on hold in order to be there for their clients whose quality of life, and often safety and security, depend on them. Living with someone who is on call 24 hours a day, seven days a week is no easy task, and our contribution would not be as rewarding, or as tolerable, without the love of those at home. Thank you.

INTRODUCTION

In my prior book, "How to Choose a Property Manager," we carefully reviewed the steps one should take in examining and assessing a property's management needs, understanding the components of a management company and preparing for and handling the interview process.

The response to "How to Choose a Property Manager" has been overwhelmingly positive. This reaction has led me to further understand the extraordinary need for materials that board members can access easily and feel comfortable relying upon with regard to dealing with the management of real property. In how many situations is someone with no hands-on experience or formal training put in a position of overseeing the operations of a multi-million-dollar entity? I can think of only one, which is serving on a volunteer board such as that of a cooperative, condominium or Homeowners Association. This is especially alarming when one takes into account that for most of us, our home is also our largest asset.

To take the above a step further, in the majority of states throughout the country there are no licensing or educational requirements for professional property managers. In reviewing the states that do have licensing requirements, you would be amazed to see that most of them do not even touch upon the basics of this industry within their licensing educational requirements. Instead, in most instances, these licensing requirements are merely a means to generate income.

In essence, not only are board members and owners with no

formal training placed in a position of overseeing the operations and planning of a multi-million-dollar entity, but they must also be able to monitor the people they hire to help them run these properties. By no stretch of the imagination am I saying that all property managers require additional training. There are many outstanding individuals out there that not only maintain the adequate knowledge and experience to operate your property but also exhibit excellent work ethics. However, as in all fields, especially those unregulated (such as property management), the consumer must have the knowledge and foresight to be able to assess and continually monitor the abilities of their service providers.

Taking all of the above into account, I felt it necessary to take "How to Choose the Right Property Manager" to the next level with this new book entitled "What to Expect from your Property Manager." You will note that the format of this book is very similar to the prior one. Each chapter deals with a different aspect of the topic, identifying not only what to look for, but how to monitor the various functions of your managing agent.

In closing, I hope you enjoy this book and find it helpful in understanding what to expect from your property manager as well as how to monitor his or her performance. It is our intention here to discuss how running a multi-million dollar property can be done by a group of volunteers in an effective and efficient manner. If that sounds like an ambitious goal, read on!

Thank you.
Leslie Kaminoff
Founder and CEO, Akam Living Services, Inc.

CHAPTER 1

BOUNDARIES OF POWERS:

Dividing Responsibilities Between the Board and the Manager

In order to achieve an understanding of what to expect from a property manager, and how you can help that manager run your property as efficiently as possible, it's important to take a look at the separation of powers between the property's board and its manager. A clear delineation of responsibilities will go a long way in avoiding misunderstandings and communication breakdowns and will help prevent problems in the long run. Accepting the role of board president or board member is an enormous commitment of time and energy. Because board members are generally untrained volunteers, the role of board member often seems like a thankless job. Most people who come up to a board member in the elevator or the lobby are not there to say, "Thank you for doing such a great job," or "I really appreciate all the late nights you put in at board meetings." No, most residents approach a board member for one reason only: to complain. "I've noticed the rugs are looking a little ratty," or, "The elevators have been really slow lately," or, "Why did the maintenance go up again this year?" are the types of refrain you'll hear constantly from fellow residents once you've made the decision to take on a board position.

But as unrewarding as it may seem at times, board members also know that they are playing a key role in assuring that the quality of life and the value of their property are being protected and looked after. Board members can—and do—make an enormous difference in how well their properties are run; they can create a positive atmosphere and cultivate a community that feels confident that their biggest personal investment is in good hands. And believe it or not, this can be done with an eye to keeping everyone's time demands to a minimum.

Board Member Responsibilities

Board member elections are held each year at the Annual Meeting. Once a resident has made the decision to run for the board, he or she notifies the residents of the property, generally by circulating a brief personal background to fellow residents. In some properties, board elections can become contentious events, with rival factions vying for control of the property. In others, apathy is so prevalent that residents must be recruited at the Annual Meeting to fill empty board seats. But whether your seat on the board is hard-earned or not, the responsibility of being a board member is not to be taken lightly.

Once the board has been established, the members must elect a hierarchy of officers, including the president, vice president, treasurer and secretary. The roles of the board members are clearly stated in each property's legal documents. In a cooperative, you'll find this information in the building's by-laws, as well as the state's Business Corporation Law (BCL). If you live in a condo, the "Condominium Declaration" will outline all the rules and regulations of the property, from the by-laws to annual meeting requirements to voting regulations, and the state's Condominium Act is the legal statute that enforces these regulations. In a Homeowners Association, the property's Declaration of Covenants and Restrictions is the legal document to follow. But regardless of the name, these guidelines must be adhered to in order to be in compliance with the legal regulations that oversee the management of jointly owned property.

It is the job of the board president to oversee all meetings, create committees and appoint committee chairs, and to set the agenda for the board. And because every president comes to the job with his or her own particular area of expertise and personal management style, every board will have its own "personality." In order to get the job done without creating an overly contentious atmosphere, a good board president must walk a fine line between conciliation and leadership. But the key to good leadership is knowing how to oversee the situation without "micromanaging." In a word: delegate. Most jobs should be assigned to committees to research and make recommendations, and every task should be handed out with an agreed-upon timetable.

The main role of the vice president is to take the place of the president if he or she is absent or unavailable. The treasurer acts as chairman of the finance committee, and holds primary responsibility for the budget. Each month, the treasurer should receive reports from the manager showing all paid bills, bank statements and reconciliations, and income received. If anything looks amiss, or doesn't match the board-approved budget, the treasurer should ask for an explanation. The treasurer also takes an active role in making decisions regarding any building investments, such as the reserve fund. The secretary is responsible for ensuring that proper minutes are kept for every meeting, itemizing the topics covered, but only in broad strokes. Too much detail can come back to haunt the board in the event of a problem. In many properties, the secretary is personally responsible for taking minutes at all meetings and keeping them on hand for future reference. Other properties prefer to hire a professional to take minutes, and some properties rely on their management company to keep track of the minutes.

In addition to understanding the various responsibilities of each board member, it's important to create a personal style that will maximize the results you are able to obtain during your tenure on the board. Don't forget that you have been elected to the board by the owners in order to represent their interests. Your fellow board members and other owners will immediately see through you if you start pushing personal agenda items, such as getting rid of that flowered wallpaper that you've always hated, or having a work-out room installed in the basement so you can drop your health club membership. Personal agendas are a great way to alienate yourself quickly from fellow board members and can lead to strange, inquisitive looks from your neighbors when you bump into them on the property.

Tony Fierimonte served for five years as board member of his Florida condominium, and in that time, he saw the demographic make-up of the property change from mostly retirees to middle-aged parents with children. "We were transitioning from mostly older people to a younger group," he recalls. "And Florida has a very multi-cultural population these days. One day I got a call from a resident complaining that no one was speaking English around the pool." As board president, Fierimonte put a stop to the restrictive new rules that had been implemented as a result of changing demographics and the influx of new residents. He found his background as a Doctor of Socio-Psychology quite useful in mediating touchy situations. While not many board members can claim such credentials, good "people skills" are a real plus when serving on a volunteer board. "You reach the point where you're tired of the same people doing the same thing over and over again," he explains. After five years, he found he was ready to move on.

But in spite of the difficulties of the job, board members can see real results of their time commitment. "When I took over, the building was falling down," says Fierimonte. "We fixed everything. We applied for grants, and our managing agent wrote them up and went to the meetings. We got funding from the county for landscaping with indigenous plants, and we won beauty awards for all the trees and flowers we put in."

It is also imperative that board members understand that they cannot act as individuals. Board decisions must be made as a team, and the team must work together during scheduled meetings. Isolating other board members and campaigning behind the scenes on specific issues is bad politics and can only lead to a divided, ineffective board. Serving on the board is like running a business, and it's important not to take things personally if they don't go your way. Even if you don't agree with a board decision, the majority must be respected. In a diverse community you will most likely have a diverse board, and thus, board members are not going to see eye to eye on every issue.

As you will learn, being on a board can be very time consuming. In addition to attending the regular meetings, one must spend time preparing for the meeting. There is always research for specific projects which may be assigned to a board member. If you are not committed, or do not have the time to attend these meetings and perform your duties as a board member, do yourself, your fellow board members and your community a favor; gracefully give up your seat. If you don't, you will be resented by your fellow board members and your minimal input will carry little, if any, weight in any decision-making process.

That having been said, if you organize your efforts, plan out your goals and the steps needed to achieve them on an annual basis, and stick to these plans, you can minimize the amount of time spent running your building, and get back to what you got on the board for in the first place: improving the quality of life and the value of each unit your are responsible for.

RULES FOR SUCCESSFUL BOARD MEMBERS

1. There is a direct correlation between organization, commitment and success. The more organized effort you put in, the more productive your term will be.

2. Run for the board for the right reasons. Leave the personal agendas at home. You're there to represent the overall community, not yourself.

3. Respect your fellow board members and the process of governing a multi-million-dollar entity.

4. Choose specific goals for your property each year, and come up with an organized plan to achieve these goals. Bring these goals and this plan to every board meeting. Keep everyone focused on the big picture when they get bogged down on the details.

Understand and abide by these four basics guidelines and you should have a productive term. Always remember that you want to improve things in your property and do it in the most efficient way possible.

Management Responsibilities

Different boards have different needs when they hire a professional manager to oversee the operations of their property. Many boards have had a history of bad experience with prior managers that led them to switch. But whether your board is seeking to improve the property's finances, update the decor or revamp the staff, there are certain things that any management company should be expected to do. The most basic is the collection of monthly maintenance fees or common charges as well as any special assessments due from every unit owner. Next, they must maintain a list of all income and expenses, create accurate monthly financial reports, inspect the property on a regular basis and see to it that all the property's income is collected on time, and that its bills are paid on time. The management firm should also oversee any capital improvement projects, obtaining bids and supervising the work.

The manager should be available to board members on a regular basis, and should also be capable of interacting with individual residents when questions or problems arise. The manager should be reachable by cell phone or beeper throughout the business day, and the company must offer 24-hour, seven-day-a-week emergency service with a response time quick enough to deal with anything from a midnight fire to a 3:00 am power outage.

While board members are expected to set policy and procedure, they should be careful not to get involved in the day-to-day operations of the property. A board member should cultivate a good rapport with the building staff, making an effort to know them by name and to be aware of their title, position and job description. But the responsibility of supervising and disciplining the staff should be left to the manager. When a board member steps into a supervisory role with staff it can only create problems. It causes a breakdown in the chain of command and the boundaries of power between the board and the manager, and can also create unnecessary tension between the staff and the board. In addition, such action may undermine the manager's authority with the staff. In order to make the manager responsible for the actions of the staff, the board must give him or her the ultimate supervisory authority. In many cases, property employees are union members, and records must be maintained in the event of a personnel problem. The management company is best equipped to document any such problems and maintain records that can be used, if necessary, to present to union officials in the unfortunate event that an employee must be terminated or disciplined.

When it comes to your property's finances, you should expect and make sure that your manager reviews and completely understands all aspects of your financials prior to you receiving your copy of this report. It is impossible to properly manage any property without having a good handle on the financials. Budgeting is another key area where a property manager and his support team must take the lead. To effectively prepare either an operational or capital budget for any property, one must have tremendous expertise in the running of real property, expense trends and accounting.

A professional manager should be prepared to write, sign and live by a contract with your board that outlines all the services the company will provide, with corresponding fees. In the best case scenario, both parties will abide by the contract, and the relationship will be successful for many years. If the marriage doesn't work out, however, management contracts should have a built-in 30-day cancellation clause that allows either party to terminate the agreement without cause.

Understanding the boundaries of power between the board and the managing agent will go a long way toward maintaining good relations and achieving common goals. A well-managed property is a team effort, and that requires time, energy and a willingness to cooperate. Knowing what to expect from your property manager from the start will help board members assess the manager's performance and communicate their needs, their praise and their dissatisfaction. Problem-solving is a huge part of running a building, as it is a part of running any business. How your board deals with the problems that arise, and how they communicate with the professional manager will make all the difference in keeping things running smoothly. Being part of the board may be, in many ways, a thankless job. But in the long run, satisfaction comes from knowing that your property is being well taken care of, and that you are improving the quality of life for everyone in your community.

CHAPTER 2

LINES OF COMMUNICATION:

Avoid Crisis Management
By Keeping in Touch

Communication has never been easier, with cell phones, Blackberry machines, PDA's and the internet, yet this is one of the biggest challenges in meeting the needs of board members. If I had $10 for every time a board member asked me in an interview, "My manager doesn't get back to me; what is your policy on call backs?"...well, you know the rest.

What is going on here is that people have misconceptions about what kind of communication is needed to run a property the right way. It is essential to put a system of communication in place that precludes the need for a board member to call a manager two or three times a week, unless there is an emergency, or there is a capital improvement project under way. Let's look at the types of communications that need to take place, and how you and your manager can streamline them and make them more effective and more time-efficient.

The Overview

The simple fact is this: we are all busy, and managers are busier than most of us. They are responsible not only to the boards of properties they manage, and to the executives at the management company they work for, but also to every resident in every property they manage. As a board member, you should try to keep your communications with everyone on your team—your fellow board members, your managing agent and the professionals you hire—short and to the point. Since board members are volunteers, many of whom work during the day, it may be best to use the technology at hand—cell phones, email or the building's website—to maintain contact with your team. It is not the quantity of contact that matters, but the quality. If you communicate effectively, you will find that you are communicating less.

Remember that you need to be organized and focused when dealing with building issues. For example, setting a policy for creating board meeting agendas is one way to maintain a line of communication and keep the meeting on topic and on time. The agenda should be put together with input from both the board president and the manager no later than a week before the board meeting. This way it can be circulated to all board members for their comments and input, and can be added to or updated before the meeting. Once the agenda has been finalized, the board's policy may be that all non-agenda items must be tabled until the next meeting. This helps focus the current meeting, while encouraging board members to be sure any future concerns are added to the agenda on time. While this may sound strict, it ensures organized, coherent, short meetings (one-and-a-half to two hours is plenty for a board meeting), makes it clear that board members need to go over the agenda before the meeting, and keeps small day-to-day items away from board meetings.

What you want to achieve is a well-run operation, one in which all facets of the property are being attended to in an organized fashion. There should be no need for crisis management, which is different from dealing with emergencies. If you and your manager are clear on what needs to get done, when, and by whom, then it should be a simple matter to check on the status of each item when you set the agenda, or during the board meeting. It may take a while for you to achieve this level of comfort, but if you and your team communicate regularly—and effectively—it can be done.

Communication is one of the key elements in maintaining good relations among board members, as well as between the board and the residents, and between the board and the manager. One of the most important strategies for avoiding problems and preventing crises is to have a well-established method by which all parties can communicate regularly. First, the board and the manager should establish a regular schedule of review and reporting for all aspects of the building, from staff management to finances to on-going maintenance projects. Knowing your manager's schedule will make it easier to keep tabs on what is going on with the building, as well as allowing the board to contact the manager easily if need be.

Your manager will carry a cell phone and/or a pager, and many make use of personal digital assistants (PDAs) for tracking their appointments, contact information and even email. Establish right off the bat what method of communication is the best for your manager, and what works best for you. While some people prefer the immediacy of a phone call, others would rather get their messages electronically when they have a moment to respond.

When problems arise and you need to reach your manager, you should expect to hear back from him or her in a reasonable amount of time. Most management companies have response times written into their contracts. For non-emergency situations, most managers will respond within three hours. For emergencies, you should have a special 24-hour, seven-day-a-week phone number where you know you will get immediate response.

Board-Manager Communication

The board and the managing agent should meet on a monthly basis. At this meeting, the manager should present to the board a complete picture of everything that has happened at the property for the past month, including a complete financial report, detailing monies collected and spent, how those figures compared to the budgeted figures for the month, and a complete explanation of any discrepancies. At the monthly meeting, the manager should also detail any actions that have occurred at the property during the month, including calls from individual owners or tenants, what they requested and how those requests were handled.

An agenda needs to be prepared for each meeting, and the board president and the manager should talk on the phone one week prior to the meeting to create this agenda. I can't stress enough the importance of the agenda; this tool enables the board to focus on the matters at hand, without getting side-tracked by tangential issues (more on the agenda in the next chapter). After each meeting, the manager should create an "Action List" of specific items the manager will accomplish by the next meeting. This action report should be distributed to each board member within 48 hours after each meeting (we will address these reports in more detail in Chapter 4).

This is obviously a lot of work, and entails the board president, the board members, and the manager being in touch during the month to prepare for the meeting, to check things off the action list, and to follow-up on action list items not yet finished. There really should be only a few reasons for the board to be in touch with the manager during the month other than to inform the manager of an incident or event that might warrant being added to the agenda. When you think of the manager-board relationship this way, it becomes clear that less, not more, communication is needed.

Now, of course, this changes when an emergency arises. We manage a building in Brooklyn Heights in New York City, which had a major fire one night. The board president called the manager, who was on the scene in two hours, with an insurance adjuster in tow. The manager worked hand in hand with the management company's disaster team and the fire and police department crews, helping to get in touch with the residents on the upper floors, and making sure everyone who needed assistance evacuating the building got the help they needed.

Once the fire was controlled, the manager called in the fire clean-up company, who began work right then and there in the middle of the night. In two days all fire damage had been removed, and by the end of the week all evacuated residents were back in their homes. In addition, thanks to the manager's attention to detail and careful documentation, all insurance company issues were handled smoothly and quickly, and not one resident had a long drawn-out negotiation with his insurance firm.

This is how a professional manager should handle emergencies—one call should be all it takes to get him to jump into action, and bring all of the professionals needed to the scene ASAP. Needless to say, this board was very pleased with the way their emergency was handled.

In another instance, a Florida condominium was hit hard by a hurricane several years ago. "The entire company worked 12 straight hours," the board president said. "It was totally unexpected, and it was the most amazing thing." Fortunately, when the hurricanes hit this year, his property was not damaged. But his experience during the last emergency was "The most positive thing that our management company could have done."

Board Member-Board Member Communication
There is little need for board members to be in touch with one another during the month, unless they are on the same committee. The exception is when the board president is putting together the agenda, and this is best handled by email and the internet. We create an internet website for each property we manage, and post minutes, proposed agendas, past committee reports and the like there for boards to access as needed. Many board members in properties we manage see each other only at meetings.

Management companies, as well as individuals, utilize the internet to varying degrees, but this can be an invaluable communication resource. The customized websites our firm sets up for each of our client properties can be accessed directly from the office or home with the click of a mouse and a password. Your property's website can provide board members with meeting minutes, committee reports, monthly financial statements, meeting agendas, and much more. In addition, board members can communicate with one another about current issues and concerns.

Residents can use the website to find out about upcoming events, to check the status of a construction or landscaping job, or, in many cases, even to pay their monthly common charges. Some properties allow residents to post "classified ads" on their websites, ranging from furniture for sale to job listings or sublets available.

And if there is a need to email out a question to be answered ASAP, we use the website to do that as well. Clear, clean lines of communication, with no need to discuss extraneous issues, makes the business of the property move forward with purpose.

Staff-Board-Manager Communication

When discussing how to deal with your staff, things get a little tricky. While it is essential to have a good rapport with supers, handymen, etc., it is also important to make sure you do not get in the way of the chain of command. All job instructions and direction must come from the manager; there is no reason for board members to give instructions to staff members. In fact, many times board and staff interaction creates conflicts with the manager's instructions to staff, and that is why this can be a difficult area.

In addition, many staff positions are filled by union members, and there are specific ways to deal with union members, especially when the board is dissatisfied with the job performance of a staff member. There are ways to terminate a union staff member, but the documentation must be specific and detailed, and you need to deal with these cases very carefully. So our advice is to be sure to communicate any problems or issues you are having with a staff member directly to the managing agent, who will document all work-related issues properly. By dealing with staff in this fashion, you reinforce the chain of command, as well as ensure that your property has the necessary documentation to bring to any formal hearings regarding a staff member. Remember, if your property manager is to be responsible for your staff's actions, he or she must be given the authority to carry out this function.

CONDUCTING PRODUCTIVE MEETINGS:

Running Your Property In a Professional Manner

I have been to board meetings where the secretary showed up in pajamas, robe and slippers. One board president insisted that we hold the October meeting in his apartment, and then proceeded to put the television on loud, so he could keep tabs on the World Series. These are not good examples of how to conduct a productive meeting, however, unfortunately, they are true stories.

We mentioned in the last chapter how important it is to have the agenda prepared in advance, and we underscore that here. If you've ever been to a long-winded, rambling board meeting that gets you home well after midnight, you know how unpleasant and unproductive they can be. Remember, the object here is that you achieve your goals on an annual basis, and you need to focus your time at each meeting to make sure you are on track to do that.

For example, we managed a building that was running a deficit each year, and was forced to constantly raise the owners' monthly fees to cover the shortfall. This practice did not sit well with the board or the residents, and one year the board decided to be forceful—they instructed us to turn around their finances. We were given the following assignment: figure out a way for us to cut spending and increase income, so that in addition to not raising our monthly fees, we can put aside a small amount—say $25,000—into our reserve funds for future repairs.

We attacked this assignment with relish, and were able to accomplish the board's stated goals by working closely with the team of professionals the board already had in place, communicating effectively (remember quality, not merely quantity) with the board, owners and residents, and keeping our eye on the goals all year long. Once we had our parameters set for the year, it made it much easier to keep everyone focused and working together to achieve what we wanted. Before we get into a few of the details of this success story, we need to remind you that one of the reasons for our success was running the board meetings properly.

Agendas are Key

It was after another annual meeting where we had to inform the residents about the need for an increase in monthly fees that the board instructed us to solve their financial problems. In order to do that, we told them, we had to put off any major repairs for the year, freeze staff bonuses, and take a few creative measures to ensure our success. The board agreed, and we set to work. The first thing the property manager did was request a meeting with the management company's Executive Committee to help with his new assignment for the year. We'll get into this in more detail in future chapters, but remember that without the proper support back in the office, no manager can achieve his or her goals.

Once we came up with a few ideas, the manager began making up the agenda for the next meeting, and put in big, bold letters right across the top: Our Goal: To Maintain Current Fees and Replenish the Reserve Fund by $25,000! Talk about keeping everyone focused—this was a great way of doing just that. And for each ensuing monthly meeting, that goal appeared right there, above the important issues to be discussed that evening.

Now with this building, it was essential that we keep all extraneous items off the agenda, because we needed all the time we had to do what we needed to do. Therefore, as we made up the agenda each month, we did not add anything about redecorating the lobby, or putting in a new elevator, or replacing the windows. Any discussion of these matters would have been a waste of time, since we had already decided we would not do any of these things! Instead, we focused on what had to be done to achieve our goal, and this is how you should handle each and every board meeting you hold for your property—with a specific focus.

We've already talked about what a good manager will prepare and bring to a monthly meeting: The monthly financial report, the action list, the income and expense report, the arrears report, the details of what happened during the month, and as I repeat this list, you can see how deeply involved the manager is in the operation of your building. The only way to keep all of this information organized and keep everyone paying attention to it is by having an agenda that makes sense.

We always begin each meeting cycle directly after a meeting, by having the manager review his notes and make a draft of the agenda for the next meeting. At the three week mark, the manager fine tunes that agenda based upon actions recently taken and sends the agenda to the board president. Once approved, the agenda goes out to all board members, and there is a comment period of a day or two. At that point the agenda is finalized, and sent around to all board members and any professionals who need to see it. (If, for example, we are discussing budget issues, we may ask the accountant to send a representative to help us explain some difficult issue to the board.)

With this agenda in hand, the manager now sets about preparing his back-up material, his monthly package (mentioned above), copies of any documentation needed for agenda items (disciplinary issues with staff, insurance queries, etc.), and a complete package for each board member. We have a fairly thick handout for each board member each month, not only for use at the meeting, but also to take home and analyze during the month, if need be. Only with the proper documentation can we help board members be prepared to execute their fiduciary responsibility to the building.

The Meeting

We encourage boards to meet at our offices, because all back-up documentation is there in files and easy to access. Most boards do take advantage of this service, but some meetings take place in the homes of one of the board members. We strongly urge boards to set out refreshments and appetizers, because after a day at work a little snack helps the board stay focused. The building can pay for this minor expense, which should cost less than $50 per meeting. We start each meeting by re-stating our current goal, and by reminding the board that any meeting that goes over an hour and a half is usually unproductive, because people begin to lose that all-important focus.

At this point we methodically run through the agenda, from top to bottom, to be sure we are following the correct rules of order, to make documentation and note-taking simple, and to give us an opportunity to begin checking off items on the list. (See sample agenda on facing page.)

The handling of the board meeting directly determines the effectiveness of the board. You can have the greatest ideas, perform incredible due diligence and have it go nowhere, if your board does not function properly. There are various ways of keeping a board on track. As you will note, your property manager must play a major role in this task. All too often I see property managers sitting at board meetings performing the duties of a secretary. This setup usually develops in situations where boards do not treat their managers as professionals, placing little or no value on their input. If you do not respect your property manager's input, do not push him aside and work around him; it is time to make a change in managers.

AGENDA
BOARD OF DIRECTORS MEETING
ABC CONDOMINIUM
JULY 31, 2004
7:00 PM IN APARTMENT #2B

1. Interview with Apartment #7N at 6:30 p.m.

2. Call meeting to order

3. Approve minutes of prior meeting (see attached)

4. Report from the Superintendent

5. Guest Speakers

6. Management Executive's Report

    A. Status of Arrears (see attached)

    B. Status of Construction Projects

7. Treasurer's Report

8. Committee Reports

9. New Business

10. Old Business

11. Schedule for next Board Meeting

12. Adjournment

KEY ELEMENTS TO AN EFFECTIVE MEETING

1. How will the meeting be run?

Most boards that are effective work under strict predetermined guidelines. As an example, the documents for many associations call for the utilization of Robert's Rules of Order. I have seen many a board totally stifled by what may be referred to as these cumbersome rules. As any trained manager will tell you, one of Robert's Rules states that it is okay to modify the rules for smaller, less formal groups. Your manager should be able to supply your board with a written document outlining the best way for an HOA, cooperative and/or condominium to utilize Robert's Rules. Your manager has the experience, let him guide your board in developing what works best for your group. Once this is accomplished it is the board president and manager's job to make sure the guidelines are strictly enforced.

2. Preparation for the meeting.

a. Agenda – it is the manager's responsibility to speak with the board president in order to develop an agenda. Your manager MUST be fully prepared to inform all board members of the various issues as well as bring various recommendations up for discussion.

b. Reports – approximately 5 to 7 days prior to your board meeting your manager should supply each board member with a written management report. The following data must be included.

- Review of all actions taken the prior month
- Documentation concerning all new items to be discussed
- Updated cash position as of the date of the meeting
- Draft of prior month's board meeting minutes
- Facilities report

By having your manager operate under the above guidelines you should have productive meetings. If you start seeing the same items linger on the agenda month after month, stop and analyze the process. While it is obviously important to address that individual issue, it is equally important to look at where it got held up along the way.

As you can see, your property manager plays a key role in assuring that the limited time your board spends together is effective. Make sure that your manager is aware of your expectations of him with regard to board meetings. The running of the board meeting is usually a weakness in most board presidents. As well it should be, unless of course the board president has prior experience in this field. Utilize your manager; he is the professional that can bring many tools to the table with regard to this topic.

CHAPTER 4

WHAT REPORTS TO EXPECT:

Financial Standards, Reporting and Investing

Cash management, financial planning and financial reporting are probably the weakest links in the operation of most management companies. This is rather frightening when one considers the fact that virtually every board decision has a financial impact on the property. By creating a set of reasonable expectations for the manager, fiscal management can be greatly improved.

Monthly Reports

When it comes to monthly reports, your board should receive monthly financial statements no later than 15 to 20 working days after the close of the month. Make sure that these reports are reconciled to the bank statements prior to being distributed to your board. In fact, it is an excellent idea to pay a visit to your management company several times throughout the year to review the reconciliations in order to assure they are up to date. Monthly financials can be provided on either a cash or accrual basis. What we recommend is that monthly reporting be prepared on a cash basis with an accrual report being generated every six months. The standard financial should include: Statements of Income and

Expenses, Accounts Payable, Accounts Receivable, Unpaid Bills and a Collection Status Report. All reports must compare actual numbers to the original prepared budget.

Every board should employ an independent accountant to ensure that the property's finances are being fully reviewed and that reporting is up to date and accurate. The accountant should make sure that the management firm's Financial Division utilizes "generally accepted accounting procedures." He should also review the qualifications of the head of the management company's financial department and make sure that the management company has outside accountants come in periodically to review their operations. In addition, the board should find out if the funds overseen by the management firm are ever commingled. Because management companies collect all the monthly common charges and maintenance fees of their client properties, funds should always be kept separate and distinct. Commingling of funds is a potential Pandora's Box of financial problems.

Within 48 hours of your monthly board meeting, all board members should receive an Action List (see sample on facing page) from the property manager. This document should be a compilation of all items the board has requested the manager deal with during the upcoming month. It is also suggested that next to each item the estimated timeframe for completion be noted. It is important that the issuance of this list to the board is timely and reviewed by all parties. By doing this there should be no surprises at the next meeting as to what was expected of the manager, the board, or the board's committees. The Action List should be reviewed by the manager's supervisor immediately to determine if any of the items require support from other individuals within the company. For example, a review of service contracts might require input by the company's Director of Operations and/or Construction. The Action List should be the key component with regard to tracking the progress of the manager during the weekly or bi-weekly meeting between the manager and his or her supervisor.

In addition to the Action List, managers should be required

ACTION LIST

PROPERTY: Harvard Condominium

MANAGER: Justin K.

DATE OF BOARD MEETING: February 19th

DATE DISTRIBUTED TO BOARD: February 20th

DATE OF NEXT BOARD MEETING: March 27th

ACTION	COMMENTS	PROPOSED COMPLETION
1) Obtain three bids for playground landscaping.	Include 32 cuts, 3 fertilizations	March 23rd
2) Revise job description for Superintendent.	To include work schedule	March 15th
3) Follow up on arrears and report to board by the 5th of each month	Include written update from attorney	Ongoing
4) Have heating units serviced for season	Complete overhaul of burner	March 3rd

to provide the board with a written Management Report three to five days prior to the monthly board meeting. This report should summarize everything the manager has accomplished over the past month in addition to including information on new agenda items to be discussed at the upcoming meeting. Prior to being distributed to board members, this report should be compared to both the minutes of the board's prior meeting and the Action List by the manager's supervisor in order to assure that nothing has fallen between the cracks.

Monthly Management Report
The Monthly Management Report (see sample report next four pages) is an excellent tool for board members, because it provides two distinct functions: First, it is an excellent way for the board to monitor the property manager's activity during the prior month. In addition, it allows board members to come to the meeting prepared to discuss and vote on the issues.

ASSOCIATES, INC.
Exceptional Management
Impeccable Reputation

8 West 38th Street, Seventh Floor
New York, New York 10018
(212) 986-0001
fax (212) 986-0002
www.akam.com

ABC CONDOMINIUM
New York, NY 10016

Monthly Board Meeting
July 31, 2004

Sample Management Report

The Meeting will commence at 7:00 P.M. in Apartment 2B, Mr. Smith

MANAGEMENT ACTIONS

The following actions related to the management of the building were taken since the last Board Meeting:

1. Interior of Building:
   Began writing spec sheet for bids on wallpaper replacement

2. Exterior of Building:
   Monitored facade cleaning

3. Preventive Maintenance:
   Serviced heating units

4. Personnel:
   Filed disciplinary action report for night doorman

5. Violations and Code Compliance:
   Installed carbon monoxide detectors in all units
   Began lead inspections

6. Alterations and Renovations:
   Reviewing architectural plans for Unit 17A kitchen renovation

7. Financial Actions:
   Reviewing reserve fund investments with financial advisor and accountant

LEGAL ACTIONS

The following details the status of legal actions commenced:

1. Non-Payment Summary Proceedings:
   Unit owner in PH2 has received notification of intent to evict

2. Illegal Sublets/Assignments:
   Owner of Unit 11C has been notified that he is in violation of building sublet policy

3. Other Legal Actions:
   Tax certiorari proceeding has been scheduled for February

4. Potential Problem Areas:
   Loose stones in entryway must be repaired to avoid injury

BUILDING IMPROVEMENT ACTIONS

Capital Improvements

At the discretion of the Board, we requested bids for the following projects (individual bid proposals are attached):

Project: Hallway Renovations
Project Detail: Replacement of carpeting, wallpaper and lighting fixtures in all hallways above the lobby floor.

	Vendor	Price
Bid #1:	The Design Specialists	$10,000 per floor
Bid #2:	High-Rise Interiors	$12,000 per floor
Bid #3	Delaney Designs	$8,500 per floor

FINANCIAL AND ACCOUNTING ACTIONS

Month Ending: *June, 2004*

OPERATING ACCOUNT: $ *63,466*

ACCOUNTS PAYABLE: $ *54,789*
(Exclusive of Mortgage,
Insurance, Taxes & Payroll)

RESERVE ACCOUNT: $ *237,559*

ASSESSMENT ACCOUNT: $ *43,500*

Site Inspection Report

At least one formal property inspection must be done every month. This should be undertaken by your manager, property superintendent and if at all possible, a member of your board or maintenance committee. Any deficiencies noted during this walkthrough should be documented. This report is a means for board members to monitor maintenance issues relating to their property. The Site Inspection Report (see sample form on opposite page) should be utilized by your manager's supervisor when doing unannounced inspections of your property.

All of these reports are helpful tools to aid boards in overseeing the management of their properties as well as assisting management companies in supervising their property managers. Therefore, it is imperative that you ascertain how, if at all, your management company utilizes these reporting systems. If your management company is not utilizing this type of data on an ongoing basis how can they be adequately supervising your property manager?

COMPREHENSIVE PROPERTY MANAGEMENT AUDIT ("CPMA")

AKAM-MANAGED PROPERTY	
AUDIT CONDUCTED BY	
DATE OF AUDIT	

AREA	GOOD	FAIR	POOR	MAINTENANCE REQUIRED
ENTRY DOOR				
Glass				
Transom				
Hinges				
Knobs and Locks				
Door Checks				
Door Finish				
Kick Plate				
Frame				
ENTRYWAY/VESTIBULE				
Security				
Housekeeping				
Ceilings				
Floors				
Door Mats				
MAILBOXES				
Doors				
Locks				
Name Plates				
Intercom				
Signal Buttons				
LOBBY				
Risers				
Steps				

AREA	GOOD	FAIR	POOR	MAINTENANCE REQUIRED
LOBBY (continued)				
Furnishings				
Doorman Station				
Doors				
Landings				
Handrails				
Walls				
Ceilings				
Floors				
Windows				
Window Coverings				
PASSENGER ELEVATORS				
Signage				
Lighting				
Leveling				
Door Operation				
Indicators				
Signal Buttons				
Doors				
Cab Floor				
Cab Ceiling				
Floor Numbers				
LAUNDRY ROOM(S)				
Walls				
Ceilings				
Floors				
Washers				
Dryers				
Vending Machines				
Tubs and Faucets				
Windows				

AREA	GOOD	FAIR	POOR	MAINTENANCE REQUIRED
LAUNDRY ROOM(S) continued				
Window Coverings				
Doors				
Vents				
COMPACTOR ROOM(S)				
Cleanliness				
Ceilings				
Floors				
Windows				
Window Coverings				
HALLWAY, REAR				
Risers				
Steps				
Landings				
Handrails				
Walls				
Ceilings				
Floors				
Windows				
Window Covering				
SERVICE ELEVATORS				
Signage				
Lighting				
Leveling				
Door Operation				
Indicators				
Signal Buttons				
Doors				
Cab Floor				
Cab Ceilings				
Floor Numbers				

AREA	GOOD	FAIR	POOR	MAINTENANCE REQUIRED
COMPACTOR ROOM – BASEMENT				
Cleanliness				
Safety Kill Switch				
Sprinkler Heads				
Hydraulic Unit				
HEATING PLANT				
Cleanliness				
Pop Safety				
Water Column				
Heat Timer Settings				
Vacuum System				
Gauges				
Insulation				
Fire Extinguishers				
Water Treatment				
Oil Filters				
Blow Down Valve				
Pre-Heaters				
SIGNAGE				
M.D.R. Number				
Superintendent				
Certificate of Occupancy				
Local Law 16 Diagrams				
Heating Plant Key				
FRONT WALL				
Base				
Top				
Surface				
Cleanliness				
SIDE WALLS				
Base				

AREA	GOOD	FAIR	POOR	MAINTENANCE REQUIRED
SIDE WALLS continued				
Top				
Surface				
Cleanliness				
REAR WALLS				
Base				
Top				
Surface				
ROOF				
Water Tank				
Tank Dunnage				
Frost Proofing				
Coping Systems				
Bulkheads				
Flashing				
Surface				
Gutters/Downspouts				
Chimneys				
Vents/Fans				
LIGHT FIXTURES				
Fixtures				
Bulbs				
Switch/Timer				
HVAC				
Chillers				
Cooling Towers				
Heat Exchanger				
MECHANICAL				
Ejector Pumps				
House Pumps				
Electric Switch Gear				

AREA	GOOD	FAIR	POOR	MAINTENANCE REQUIRED
MECHANICAL continued				
Gas Service				
Standpipe				
Hot Water Circulation				
GROUNDS				
Soil				
Grass				
Shrubs				
Flowers				
Trees				
Sprinklers				
Walks				
Parking and Curbs				
Driveway				
Fences				
Signs				
Trash Containers				
SWIMMING POOL				
Pump				
Motors				
Deck Area				
Tile				
Fence				
Signs				
Lockers				
Dressing Rooms				
Sauna				
HEALTH CLUB				
Floors				
Mirrors				
Equipment				

AREA	GOOD	FAIR	POOR	MAINTENANCE REQUIRED
HEALTH CLUB continued				
Walls/Wall Coverings				
Lighting				
Ceiling				
Vents				
Cleanliness				
Bathroom				
Windows				
Window Coverings				
TENNIS COURT				
Playing Surface				
Nets				
Fence				
Covers				
Signs				
ADDITIONAL COMMENTS:				

Budget Planning

Expect your manager and his financial support team to prepare both day-to-day operating and capital budgets for you. These should be detailed, including a comparison to last year's actual as well as footnotes defining how the numbers were derived. On a monthly basis you should receive a report showing exactly where you stand relative to your budget. Any and all significant variances should be analyzed and presented to you immediately. Find out who will be responsible for supplying you with this information, when to expect it each month and what the format will be.

In most management companies a team of professionals handles the task of preparing budgets. This team generally includes your property manager, the Vice President of Operations (or comparable position) and the Chief Financial Officer. They should do the following:

Recap of current year: Review all income and expense items (actual versus budget) for the previous year, or nine months due to the fact that the budgeting process usually begins three months prior to the end of your fiscal year. This is a good time to examine potential increases in income or reduction of expenses. This analysis should be documented with explanations for variances and/or suggestions for the upcoming year. For example, look for underutilized space in your property, which may be converted into a source of revenue.

Identify upcoming changes and project their effects: There are certain items that are going to affect your upcoming budget which your manager should have a strong handle on. Therefore, it should be reasonably easy to identify the financial impact each of these items will have on your upcoming budget. Some of the areas I am referring to are contractual labor agreement increases, service contract rate increases, increases in taxes due to the loss of an abatement, energy savings due to upgrading and/or the replacement of equipment.

Expense Forecast: Review all recurring expenses and project appropriate increases. One of the best ways of doing this is by contacting the facilitator of the service or vendor of the supplies and get their input. All forecasted expenses must be footnoted with an explanation of how the number was derived. This will assist tremendously when trying to analyze any variances in the future.

Now that your budget committee has been supplied with the above data, and has had a chance to analyze and question the information, it is time for your manager to put all the pieces together and present a first draft of your upcoming fiscal year's budget. For ease of working with these numbers we recommend that they be put together and presented in the following format:

Categories: List all budgetary items separated by income and expenses. The more detailed your budget is the easier it will be to work with during the upcoming year. For example, you can have one category entitled Utilities, or break that down into the following subcategories: oil, gas, and electricity. Obviously, the more detailed your expenses are broken down the easier it will be to identify and analyze any variances.

First nine months actual: This column should indicate the Exact income and expenditure for each category for the first nine months of the property's operations.

Months ten through 12 projected: Based upon the first nine months of actual data, the remaining three months of the fiscal year must be projected.

Current year projected totals: These numbers represent nine months of actual figures plus your three months of projections.

Current year's budget: This column notates your original budget numbers for the current year.

Variances between current budget and projected year-end: Comparison of current budget and where you are projecting to end the year. All major variances must be analyzed.

Upcoming year's budget: In composing this data we examine

expense items first taking the following into account for each category.

- Review of current year-end projections

- Analysis of any variance between projected year-end and original budget

- Review of expense forecast for the upcoming year in all categories showing variances from original projection

Taking all of the above data into consideration, compute a number for your upcoming year's budget. Make sure that each entry has an accompanying footnote explaining how the number was derived. (See sample budget on facing page.)

By having your management team perform the budget process as indicated above, all board members should have an excellent understanding of all income and expense items. Just throwing together numbers, without performing all the above outlined steps, will only create future problems. Proper budget preparation is essential in order to work effectively with your numbers throughout the year.

Investment Strategies

When it comes to the reserve fund and any other funds that need to be invested, your board should be able to rely on the Chief Financial Officer of the management company to assist you in making prudent investment decisions. Make sure that the individual giving you investment advice is experienced and has a proven track record. Remember, this is property money, not your own. Our advice is to take limited risks when investing, and to take absolutely no risk with regard to principal.

One board we work with has a reserve fund of over $250, 000. Since they feel strongly that these funds must be invested carefully, they bought two separate U.S. Treasury Bills for $100,000 each, which generate somewhere in the 3% to 4% range. This does not generate very much, but the $6,000 to $8,000 which these investments throw off adds to the reserve fund annually, and the

BUDGET 2002

	ACTUAL 1999	ACTUAL 2000	BUDGET 2001	ESTIMATED ACTUAL 2001	BUDGET 2002
INCOME					
Maintenance	652,183	680,684	684,472	695,400	700,462
Commercial Rent	28,200	36,850	40,200	0	0
Late Fees	2,692	1,983	2,400	1,500	1,500
Sublet fees	850	14,600	9,000	15,550	0
Assessment	0	0	0	33,860	37,760
Interest Income	0	16,647	18,000	18,040	18,000
Flip Tax	0	5,900	6,000	1,000	1,000
Misc. Income	1,197	1,328	1,200	740	1,000
TOTAL INCOME	**685,122**	**757,992**	**761,272**	**766,090**	**759,722**
EXPENSES					
FINANCIAL					
Mortgage	147,101	147,101	147,101	147,100	147,100
Water & Sewer	12,933	13,062	13,700	13,700	14,385 **(A)**
R/E Taxes	162,157	186,216	198,979	213,610	222,140 **(B)**
Corporate Taxes	2,897	1,468	4,000	4,290	5,000
TOTAL FINANCIAL	**325,088**	**347,847**	**363,780**	**378,700**	**388,625**
PAYROLL					
Bonus	6,475	2,125	4,000	4,000	4,000
Gross	25,126	28,666	24,800	34,090	35,130 **(C)**
Payroll Taxes	2,087	2,311	2,017	2,990	2,800 **(D)**
Health/Welfare	5,194	7,070	6,000	6,300	6,000 **(E)**
W/C DBL	452	755	1,200	460	500
Misc. Payroll	672	1,272	1,200	730	1,000
TOTAL PAYROLL	40,006	42,199	39,217	48,570	49,430
OPERATING					
Electricity and Gas	16,237	17,877	24,000	24,800	26,040 **(F)**
Supplies	2,407	2,668	3,600	4,460	5,000
Exterminator	244	379	325	350	350
Security	108,013	148,554	141,600	143,580	147,380
Permits	78	181	500	10	100
Misc. Operating	298	0	1,500	550	1,000
TOTAL OPERATING	127,277	169,659	171,525	173,750	179,870

BUDGET 2002

	ACTUAL 1999	ACTUAL 2000	BUDGET 2001	ESTIMATED ACTUAL 2001	BUDGET 2002
REPAIRS & MAINTENANCE					
Elevator	2,819	3,927	3,600	3,750	3,700
Plumbing	2,875	5,171	6,000	5,150	6,000
Roof	0	1,898	1,200	1,000	1,200
Electrical	1,320	0	1,000	800	1,000
Door/Lock	2,354	179	0	1,990	1,000
Landscape/Garden/Flowers	4,719	6,153	12,000	8,130	8,500
Compactor/Incinerator	0	0	0	1,290	1,500
Misc. Repairs & Maint.	4,906	6,842	7,500	9,980	8,000
TOTAL REPAIRS & MAINTENANCE	18,993	24,170	31,300	32,090	30,900
ADMINISTRATIVE					
Insurance	16,100	15,668	16,559	16,990	21,238 (G)
Legal	10,000	8,167	2,187	1,340	2,000
Engineer / Architect	1,800	1,720	0	1,080	1,000
Professional Fees	400	424	400	1,360	1,000
Accounting	3,600	5,224	3,266	5,050	5,000
Management Fees	19,500	18,728	18,007	19,480	20,260
Telephone	1,000	821	874	950	1,000
Beeper	120	121	120	120	130
Membership Dues	150	135	321	140	200
Messenger/Courier	250	249	177	500	500
Postage	600	525	688	990	800
Duplicating	1,500	1,319	1,277	1,160	900
Bank Charges	600	564	1,118	560	400
Faxing	250	145	173	250	250
Misc. Administration	1,000	468	903	590	1,000
TOTAL ADMIN.	**56,870**	**54,278**	**46,070**	**50,560**	**55,678**
TOTAL EXPENSES	**568,234**	**638,153**	**651,892**	**683,670**	**704,503**
OPERATING SURPLUS / (DEFICIT)	**116,888**	**119,839**	**109,380**	**82,420**	**55,219**
					−7.88%

PROPOSED BUDGET ASSUMPTIONS
2002

(A)   WATER & SEWER

2001 Actual + 5%

(B)   REAL ESTATE TAXES

	Taxable Value	Tax Rate	2002 Annual Tax
2001/2002	1,923,300		
2002/2003	2,019,465	11.000%	222,141.15

The 02/03 assumes 5% increase in assessed value and a tax rate of 11 %

(C)   PAYROLL

		Hourly		Increased Hourly		Total
			26 weeks		26 weeks	
Super	1	15.38	16,000	15.98	16,624	32,624
	1		16,000		16,624	32,624
					@ 56 weeks	35,134

(D)   PAYROLL TAXES

FICA		35,134	X	0.0765	=	2,688
FUTA	1	7,000	X	0.008	=	56
SUI	1	8,500	X	0.007	=	60
						2,803

(E)   HEALTH

HEALTH	1	X	6,000	=	6,000
					6,000

(F)   GAS / ELECTRIC

Prior year actual plus 5% increase.

(G)   INSURANCE

2001 Estimated Actual plus anticipated 25% increase for 2002

safety of the investments is beyond question.

The board takes the remaining money, and the money from the T-bills (which are only insured up to $100,000), and leaves it in a money market fund, which has a low interest rate (currently around 1%), so that money can be accessed quickly if need be. We encourage you to consider this type of safe, secure investing, and avoid speculating with the financial underpinnings of your property.

CHAPTER 5

MANAGER-BOARD RELATIONS:

Who Does What and How

Understanding the responsibilities of each member of the management team, both the volunteer board and the professional manager and his supervisors and support staff, will increase your chances of having a positive management experience. Jay Bloomfield, who has served on the board of his Upper West Side Manhattan co-op for three years as president and nine as treasurer, had the unique experience of helping transform the building from a rental to a cooperative.

"It was our job to hire the building's first manager after the conversion," he explains. After an extensive search, the board chose one of Manhattan's top management companies. They liked the firm, but, "We were unhappy with our account executive. So we went to the principals of the company and they immediately replaced the agent." As it turned out, it took one more turn-over before his board found a compatible manager. "The third one we really like," says Jay. "He's been with us for eight years now."

Jay's board made two good decisions during this process: they searched extensively until they found a company that they liked, and then, when they were unhappy with the manager assigned to them, they worked with the company principals to solve the problem. Rather than blaming the company, they realized the problem was with the individual account executive.

"Attention to detail, following up on current projects, making good recommendations, and telling you what you don't know," are some of the things Jay's board expects from their manager. Style is also important, such as how the manager relates to the board members, whether he or she answers calls promptly and treats board members with respect. Personalities and management styles have to blend well, or the relationship won't return optimum results.

One problem that many managing agents face is an overwhelming workload. "Ten properties is too much for one person to handle," advises Jay. "We had a lot of construction work to be done, and when you are getting bids, referring contractors and negotiating contracts, it can be overwhelming. Our manager handles five or six properties, so he can devote more time to each." Of course, the work load depends not only on the number of properties your agent handles, but on the type of property. Now that Jay's property has been a co-op for twelve years, most of the heavy work has been done and things function smoothly. "We meet maybe nine times a year and meetings last about an hour," he says. The board gets along, sets policy, oversees the manager and lets the agent do his job. Properties whose boards tend to disagree and micro-manage will take much more of the agent's time, as will those properties that have a lot of capital improvements in the works.

Corporate Structure

In order to get the most out of your managing agent, and to successfully correct problems that arise, it is important to understand how the management company operates both structurally and inter-personally. Let's take a look at the corporate structure of your firm. Will you be dealing with a corporation, partnership, public or private entity? Is there more than one owner? If so, are they all active in the business? What are their backgrounds? Believe it or not, this information is crucial in understanding how your individual manager will relate to your property. Corporate philosophy flows downward; in essence the company's leaders dictate the culture of the entity. More frequently than not, a company's strengths and weaknesses relate directly to the principals' strengths and weaknesses. For instance, if the company is owned and operated by an individual with 15 years of financial experience, who has never actually managed the day-to-day operations of a property, you would probably find that this company would have a strong back office but may be lacking in the operations end of the business. A company with a well-rounded CEO who has surrounded himself with key professionals specializing in the various disciplines, such as finance, construction, training, etc. will be able to excel in all the necessary areas.

You may also find that in a privately held company it is easier to get individualized attention than in a publicly held company that may have interests elsewhere. In any case, the structure of a management company has a direct impact on the ability of your manager to perform his job. In an effort to optimize your management relationship, it also helps to understand the structure of the organization you are involved with. What is the chain of command? How many layers are there between the manager and the owner of the company? Your management company should provide you with a copy of their table of organization. If they cannot give you one, or ask for a few days to prepare one for you, it may mean that the company is not organized well internally, a situation in which even the most well-organized manager could not succeed.

Your board should also know what, if any, administrative, financial, and operational support is available to your agent. What are the qualifications of the support team? What is the ratio between upper level support staff and managers and back office staff and managers? The most highly qualified people can be placed in support positions, however, if the ratio between support staff and managers is too high, their ability to perform is dramatically diminished.

When initially assessing a management company, a good

question to ask is what their retention rate is. Client retention relates directly to a service company's ability to alter their operations to meet the needs of their clients. You should also know what educational requirements the company insists on prior to hiring an individual, and if they offer their managers and property staff any continuing education opportunities. If you expect your manager to be proactive, then the firm they work for must be proactive with regard to continuing education. In today's world, the way we do business is changing daily. There are new laws constantly being promulgated regarding the management of real property as well as new techniques developing with regard to maintaining property. If the management firm does not take an active role in educating its staff, you may find that before long, they are using outmoded technology and systems.

The Back Office

One of the fastest-changing areas in the business of real property management is the technological arena. Be sure that your management firm offers adequate technology for your manager to perform his or her duties. Do they provide cell phones, email and laptops for each management executive? What type of software does the manager have on his or her computer? Is it adequate to prepare spreadsheets or data analysis as may be needed? Does your management company offer your property any technology such as a customized website to post minutes, bulletins, schedules, upcoming events, financial data, etc? Is there a computer professional on staff at the management company to assist with this technology? It's imperative that your manager has the tools by which to supply you with the information required to make educated choices.

In addition, it is crucial that your manager have a clean, neat and organized work environment. Visit the management company, walk the office. If you observe chaos and/or a lack of enthusiasm by the employees, remember that these attitudes may be reflected in your manager. All of us require structure and support at our workplace. Without this, we will never be able to perform optimally.

Response

Property management is the ultimate personalized service business. If homeowners cannot get through to a responsible party at the management office or calls do not get returned promptly, the relationship will never work. Does your firm have an automated attendant or an actual human being answering all calls? Personally, I feel that when owners call a management company, they deserve a live voice on the other end of the line. After all, everyone's time is valuable and no one wants to get lost in a web of voice mail commands.

It is not unreasonable to expect a return phone call from the management office within two hours. Returning calls can be monitored several different ways. With today's technology, there are many phone systems that automatically track all incoming and outgoing calls by extension. These systems also have the ability to produce reports, which should be monitored on a regular basis by the management company's executive level. After a few months of review, the management company should have a good idea of what the ratio of incoming to outgoing calls should be on any given month. If a drastic deviation appears, it should be investigated immediately. If the management company does not have this technology, there are other methods of tracking, such as phone logs. Each member of the management company's staff should be required to maintain a log (see sample log on following page) in which every incoming and outgoing call is logged, including notes as to what the call was in reference to. As a board member, you should insist that these logs be brought to all board meetings for your review.

Insurance

You should also be familiar with the kinds of insurance that your management company holds. In addition to the standard liability and worker's compensation insurances that every business should maintain, the following are essential coverages that companies dealing in the management of real property should carry for each property they manage:

PHONE LOG

DATE	NAME	TELEPHONE	MESSAGE	CALL RETURNED
10/6/04	Joe Smith, BP 301645	679-1318	please call re new lead law	10/6/04
10/6/04	Delaney Designs	255-1767	re bid on ABC Condo	
10/6/04	Art Simpson, Acct.	643-9797	re ABC Condo audit	
10/6/04	Art Simpson		audit is underway — web 10/20	
10/7/04	Connie Jones, BP 9w.4th	456-7890	needs new manager	10/7/04
10/7/04	Kathy McCausland	617-1953	Super didn't show up	10/7/04
10/7/04	John O'Brien E96	246-2000	no heat in building	10/7/04
10/7/04	King oil Co.	369-1100	check boiler at E96	
10/7/04	John Boyleston	x.10	call E96 + fix heat prob	

Fidelity Bond (Crime Policy) – Amount of coverage should be at least equal to the sum of all your reserve funds, operating funds and security deposits (if applicable). Find out which employees are covered by the policy.

Professional Liability Coverage (Errors & Omissions) – Depending on the size and complexity of your property we recommend limits of $1,000,000 to $5,000,000.

Make sure that all your management firm's insurance policies are written with "A" rated carriers and that your property is listed as an insured party. While you are reviewing your management company's insurance, it might be the opportune time to ask if they have ever had any claims paid on either of the above policies. If the answer is yes, investigate the matter to determine what exactly happened and what has been done to ensure that the same thing doesn't happen again.

CHAPTER 6

MANAGING PROPERTY STAFF:

Organizational Structure, Responsibilities and Communication

Human Resources is one of the most important functions that your property manager handles. Without a good team working on a property, there is no way any board can succeed in improving the quality of life for all residents, as well as increasing values. The selection, supervision and training of your staff is a key aspect in making sure that your property shows well on the outside as well as having its internal components maintained properly. Each and every property is unique when it comes to staffing. With that in mind, the tasks of hiring, training and supervision must be developed and implemented by your property manager specifically for your site.

While your property manager may have an outline of techniques to be utilized in this area, make sure that the programs themselves are being developed to be site specific, that is, for your property alone. Prior to the implementation of any such programs, your board should be presented with written guidelines outlining the goals and objectives of the plan as well as the technique to be used for implementation.

Hiring

The first step in hiring any employee is to create a Job Outline. This outline should consist of three sections: Job Eligibility Requirements, Job Description and Compensation and Benefits Summary. The Job Outline (see following pages) must be prepared with great consideration and foresight with regard to all aspects of the functions which will make up this job. This will not only be a guide for the hiring process, but will also be utilized in annual performance reviews of the employee.

The Job Outline should list the requirements for applying for this job, including education, work experience and, if applicable, any license requirements. The Job Description (sample on following page) should include a schedule of duties as well as performance requirements. Duties should be outlined as specifically as possible. However, in order to protect the employer, a clause such as the following should be included: "and any additional duties your supervisor may assign you from time to time." The training which will be made available to the newly hired employee should also be outlined in this document. Include a time frame in which you expect the employee to be at an acceptable level of performance.

The Compensation and Benefits Summary should outline policies with regard to vacation time, sick days and holidays. It should also discuss compensation with regard to starting salary, review process and raises. This is also a good time to review the disciplinary process utilized by the employer.

Training

The key to maintaining a proficient staff is training. Your manager must design and implement training programs for each job description specifically for your property. Where most managers fail in this area is that they do not understand that training must be an ongoing process. In other words, training staff members when they initially take on their responsibilities will not provide the long-term effects a demanding board and its residents are looking for. The most effective training includes refresher programs which take

CONDOMINIUM RESIDENT MANAGER RESPONSIBILITIES

The purpose of this document is to state the responsibilities of the Resident Manager of _____Condominium. This document is not intended to be all-inclusive and does not reflect every detail of the Resident Manager's professional responsibilities and obligations. The duties and responsibilities are as follows:

The Resident Manager shall supervise all building staff, provide adequate instruction to all building staff members to ensure that their duties are performed properly; ensure that all building staff members are carrying out their duties and responsibilities and that their appearance is up to standard; conduct periodic meetings with each building staff member regarding job performance; assign additional duties as required; and coordinate the job duties and responsibilities of any absent employee as necessary.

The Resident Manager shall be knowledgeable about, comply with, and ensure building staff compliance with all building House Rules, policies and procedures, and shall conduct semi-annual meetings with all building staff in order to review all such House and Staff rules, policies, and procedures.

The Resident Manager shall attend all regularly scheduled monthly meetings of the Board of Directors and all Annual Meetings of the condominium; and shall provide to AKAM, in writing and at least one week in advance of the meeting, any items to be included on that meeting's agenda.

The Resident Manager shall cooperate fully and in the spirit of teamwork with AKAM.

The Resident Manager shall ensure the security, cleanliness, proper maintenance, and operation of all aspects of the building, including but not limited to the structural, mechanical, and aesthetic conditions of the common areas, lobbies, Health club, elevators, mechanical rooms, roof, walkways, and compactor rooms; inspect the interior and exterior portions of the building on a daily basis and note all conditions that require the attention of the building staff, including but not limited to ensuring that all walkways are free of trip hazards, debris, and snow and ice; and report any problems to AKAM.

The Resident Manager shall monitor the heat, hot water, and ventilation systems of the building on an ongoing basis; shall ensure that all required maintenance as recommended by the manufacturer is performed; and shall report all malfunctions to the service company.

The Resident Manager shall ensure the viability of the building's water towers, including ensuring that regular inspections are performed for leaks and structural integrity, and that all deficiencies are corrected. The Resident Manager shall ensure that monthly standpipe inspections are performed, and that the Monthly Standpipe Inspection Report is completed, kept on file, and a copy provided to AKAM. The Resident Manager shall ensure that the building's plumbing is in good working order; shall schedule all plumbing-related repairs; and shall ensure that all plumbing-related repairs are performed properly and timely.

The Resident Manager shall ensure the smooth and uninterrupted operation of the building elevators, and shall ensure that all elevator malfunctions are reported to the service company.

The Resident Manager shall ensure that all routine and emergency calls from shareholders or tenants are responded to promptly, efficiently, and completely by building staff.

The Resident Manager shall perform a weekly inspection to ensure that the building has all cleaning, repair, and maintenance supplies necessary for proper building maintenance, and shall order needed supplies only through approved vendors.

The Resident Manager shall ensure that the handling and removal of trash from the building is done properly and in compliance with all laws and regulations; shall monitor the condition of the trash removal equipment in the service courtyard area; and shall arrange for the appropriate removal of all debris from that area. The Resident Manager shall ensure that building staff maintain all public areas with working light bulbs as required.

The Resident Manager shall coordinate apartment access for all appropriate and authorized vendors requiring such access for exterior, interior, and all other building projects, including but not limited to coordination of apartment access for water testing and other work as may be required to be performed by the building's consultants, engineers, and/or architects.

The Resident Manager shall supervise all building-wide projects, including but not limited to exterior restoration projects; and the Resident Manager shall monitor alterations on a weekly basis and provide to AKAM on a monthly basis a written status report when necessary, of all apartment alterations ongoing in the building. The Resident Manager shall monitor all individual resident repairs performed in the building by outside contractors; and shall provide to AKAM an updated list of all types of work ongoing in any resident apartment. The Resident Manager shall ensure the apartment-by-apartment tracking of all major interior and exterior repairs.

The Resident Manager shall ensure the security of all keys to resident apartments, and shall enforce the rule that no apartment key shall be given to anyone unless specifically authorized in writing by the resident; and shall cause a key log to be maintained for keys that are received from residents for pick-up by others.

The Resident Manager shall report to AKAM all visits to the premises by any Fire Department, Sanitation Department, Building Department, or other inspector; and shall immediately forward to AKAM all paperwork left by the inspector.

The Resident Manager shall contact approved vendors for repairs and other services as required in the building and/or as requested by AKAM and help obtain and review estimates. The Resident Manager shall routinely review and authorize payment, as appropriate, of all vendor bills.

The Resident Manager shall prepare all building staff member weekly payroll time sheets; monitor all building staff allowable vacation sick, personal, and clinic days on an employee-by-employee basis;

and shall submit to AKAM timely and accurate time sheets and a report of each employee's taken vacation, sick, personal, and clinic days.

The Resident Manager shall immediately report to AKAM any major problems occurring in the building and/or with the building staff; and shall report to AKAM in writing all accidents or injuries that occur on the premises, including any that involve staff, resident, vendors, and/or guests.

The Resident Manager shall attend all employee grievance hearings, New York City code enforcement hearings, court appearances, and/or any other events requiring his attendance during regular business hours.

The Resident Manager shall be available and on-call for building emergencies at all times, without exception, including after normal working hours (unless other arrangements have been made in advance to effect the necessary coverage); shall be reachable by phone, cell phone, pager, or other reasonable means at all times; and shall at all times inform the designated building staff member of his whereabouts whenever he is out of the building. The Resident Manager shall advise AKAM if he is unable to report for work so that appropriate coverage can be arranged. The Resident Manager shall provide advance written requests to the AKAM Management Executive regarding desired personal time and/or vacation time.

_____

Signed by

_____

Date

AKAM LIVING SERVICES, Inc.
Exceptional Services for the Discerning Homeowner

FOR ALL BUILDING STAFF MEMBERS

As a Building Staff Member of The 155 Condominium, it is expected that you will:

Take pride in the quality of your work.

Do your work with an attitude of cooperation and courtesy.

Follow the orders of the Superintendent and, in the absence of the Superintendent, the orders of the Handyman, in the performance of your duties.

I. i)   About Your Work Day...

(1)   Begin work on time and stay for the full duration of your assigned shift. Do not leave the building during your shift except if you are taking your permitted lunch break.

(2)   Be dressed in your uniform as soon as your shift begins, and remain in your uniform throughout your shift.

(3)   Stay in your assigned work area. Do not leave your assigned work area without permission from your immediate supervisor, and do not loiter in any area of the building, including the lobby area and the Concierge Desk, at any time before, during, or after your shift.

(4)   Take your scheduled break only at the specified time and only in the locker room.

(5)   Do not read, listen to the radio (unless authorized by the Super at a low volume) or watch television while you are on duty.

(6)   Do not take or receive telephone calls while on duty except when necessary and not often. The only exception is the Doorman, who may use the telephone in the performance of his duties, such as assisting a resident in getting a taxi or limousine.

(7)   Do not eat or drink any food in the lobby area, elevators, or any of the public areas of the building.

(8)   No Building Staff Member is permitted to smoke anywhere in the building.

(9)   Report any and all unusual and/or suspicious occurrences

or conditions to the Superintendent immediately. This includes but is not limited to damage to or marring of the building's public areas, elevators, etc.

(10) Leave the building promptly at the end of your shift. Do not socialize or interfere in any way with any co-worker who is still working at the end of your shift.

(11) Change shifts with co-workers only with the prior approval of the Superintendent. There are no exceptions to this rule.

(12) If you are unable to report to work due to illness or for a personal reason, you must notify the Superintendent at least four (4) hours in advance by calling his office. If he does not answer leave a message on his answering machine. This is to give the Superintendent enough time to arrange to cover the shift(s) you will be missing.

I. ii) About Communication.....

(1) Be discreet. Do not talk to anyone about any resident living in the building, and do not give out any information regarding any resident. The names of the residents are confidential and are not to be shared with anyone for any reason. Refer all such inquiries to Management.

(2) In writing, report all suggestions and complaints from residents to the Superintendent along with a copy to the Board as soon as you can.

(3) Discuss any observations you have about how the building is run, and/or any complaints about hours, work assignments, or disciplinary actions, with the Superintendent or Management only. These issues are not to be discussed with residents under any circumstances.

(4) Tell the Superintendent whenever your home address and/ or telephone number changes. You will be held responsible if you cannot be contacted because you failed to inform the Superintendent of a change in your personal contact information.

I. iii) Remember That.....

(1) Your personal appearance is important to your job. The uniform that has been provided to you is not to be worn at

any time except during your assigned shift. At the end of your shift, your uniform is to be carefully and neatly hung in the locker room. The condominium has made provisions for the cleaning and pressing of Concierge uniforms, and the changing of Handyman and Porter uniforms, on a regular basis. If you notice any defect in your uniform, report it to the Superintendent immediately so that it can be corrected in time for your next shift.

(2)   In addition to taking proper care of your uniforms, it is expected that you will come to work clean and well groomed every day. This means that you should shower and shave daily, your hair should be neat, your hands and fingernails should be clean, and your shoes should be shined.

(3)   At no time are controlled illegal substances to be taken by, or be in the personal possession of, or in the locker of, any Building Staff Member. Also, it is not permitted to arrive at work intoxicated, or impaired in any way due to an illegal controlled substance, nor is it permitted to become intoxicated or impaired in any way at any time you are in the building. Failure to abide by these rules will subject you to immediate discharge as sanctioned by the Union.

(4)   At no time are weapons of any kind, either registered or unregistered, to be brought into or stored in the building by any Building Staff Member. This includes guns, knives, razors, box cutters, mace, or any other instrument that may be construed as a weapon. Failure to abide by this rule will subject you to immediate discharge as sanctioned by the Union.

I. iv)   A Final Note.....

(1)   Your continued employment in the building depends on you. To avoid disciplinary action, including warnings, suspension, and discharge, always do your work properly, conscientiously, and with the appropriate attitude toward the building, the Superintendent, Management, your co-workers, and building residents and their visitors.

place every six to twelve months depending on the staff.

Another shortfall in most training programs is that the context deals only with the specific functions for which the staff is responsible. In order to provide your property with a truly effective staff, many areas, from appearance to communication, must be addressed. Each member of your building staff must be made aware of the fact that his physical appearance and the neatness of his work area will have a huge impact on how he is perceived by his employer as well as individual homeowners. Personnel should also be instructed on how to communicate with the residents. For instance, unit owners and their guests should not be greeted with "Hey, how are you?" A simple, "Good morning, Mr. Wells," is a lot more pleasant. In short, training must be repetitive and all-encompassing, and nothing should be taken for granted.

Disciplinary Action

Since your property manager is the person who will be in charge of the hiring and supervision of your staff, it is only fitting that he implement and oversee your Disciplinary Policies and Procedures. These procedures must be well documented and distributed to all employees along with a copy of their job description and schedule upon the commencement of their employment. It is essential that whatever the disciplinary procedures, that they are utilized in the exact same way for all employees. Failure to do so may lead to major labor relations problems.

Those properties that employ union personnel must adhere to the sections of the respective union contract which deal with this issue. It is your manager's responsibility to have a thorough understanding of the union contract. I have seen managers terminate employees for various acceptable reasons and then have to take them back to work because they did not follow the union contract guidelines for disciplinary action.

Those buildings that do not employ union workers should create their own set of guidelines. Following is a suggested procedure:

Employee Disciplinary Report ™

akam
ASSOCIATES, INC.

Copy to: ☐ Employee ☐ Employee's Personnel Representative ☐ Other _____

Name _____ Division _____

ID# _____ Department _____

Date of Incident _____ Time of Incident _____

Action to be taken: ☐ Warning ☐ Suspension ☐ Dismissal

This report is to be made part of the official record of the above-mentioned employee.

Nature of incident:

☐ 1. Unexcused Absence
☐ 2. Tardiness
☐ 3. Drinking while on duty
☐ 4. Insubordination
☐ 5 Dishonesty
☐ 6. Use of illegal drugs while on duty
☐ 7. Failure to follow instructions
☐ 8. Fighting on company premises
☐ 9. Leaving without permission
☐ 10. Substandard work

☐ 11. Housekeeping
☐ 12. Improper conduct
☐ 13. Reporting under the influence of alcohol
☐ 14. Violation of safety rules
☐ 15. Carelessness
☐ 16. Destruction of company property
☐ 17. Defective and improper work
☐ 18. Violation of company rules of conduct
☐ 19. Theft
☐ 20. Other _____

Supervisor's remarks: _____
_____
_____

Witnesses: _____

Employee's Remarks: _____
_____
_____

☐ Probationary Employee

Signature of Supervisor _____ Date _____

I have read this report.

Signature of employee _____ Date _____

The above offense or offenses have been noted and are made a part of the above employee's personnel file as of this date.

Offense Number ☐ 1 ☐ 2 ☐ 3 ☐ 4 ☐ 5

Last Offense Date _____

Additional remarks: _____
_____
_____

Personnel Department Signature _____ Date _____

First Infraction: Have a face-to-face conference with the employee. Go over the specific infraction and make sure that he completely understands where he went wrong and how to avoid it in the future. Document your meeting with a memo from you to the employee's file.

Second Infraction: Repeat the above procedure with the addition of handing the employee a written warning notice and advising him that any further infractions on his part will lead to a suspension.

Third Infraction: Provide a written warning notice for the employee with a three to five-day suspension. The warning notice should indicate that any further infractions will lead to immediate termination.

The above procedure can be managed easily with the use of a preprinted warning notice, such as the Employee Disciplinary Report shown on the previous page.

Staff Meetings and Formal Reviews
Maintaining a professional staff is no different from coaching any winning team. You can have the best-made plans and most desirable staff, but if they don't work as a team you will not succeed. It is the job of your manager to steer the staff in the right direction. He must adequately maintain motivation. Some techniques which should be utilized are regular staff meetings, individual meetings, routine performance reviews and rewards for good performance.

Job reviews should cover all aspects of job performance and should be conducted at least once a year, preferably twice a year. During the job review process, the Account Executive should sit down privately with each staff member and rate each aspect of his or her performance according to a scale such as the one on the Superintendent's Performance Evaluation on the following pages. If there are areas of under-achievement, the employee should be notified, and a detailed explanation should be offered on how to improve the level of performance.

When staff members are union employees, annual pay increases may be mandated by their contract. Otherwise, pay raises are at the discretion of the property, and should be decided upon based on performance evaluation, length of duty, and other criteria. Holiday bonuses are customary in December, and again, should be based on performance, seniority, and other criteria determined by the board and the property manager.

Job Responsibilities

Job descriptions, employee handbooks, and standards for review are essential elements in keeping property staff trained, informed and satisfied. All of these documents will also help keep your staff happy with their work environment, because there is nothing more stressful to employees than not knowing what is expected of them or how they are viewed by their employers. A clearly outlined hierarchy of jobs and responsibilities will also improve performance and will help minimize misunderstandings between staff members. Maintaining a regular schedule for each employee will keep overtime to a minimum as well as allowing each staff member to put in vacation requests early, plan for personal time off, and establish a regular working schedule.

SUPERINTENDENT PERFORMANCE EVALUATION

Name:	Anthony Mahony	
Time in position:		Review Date:

INSTRUCTIONS: For each relevant category, circle the appropriate box. If a category is not relevant, do not circle and move to the next category.

	CATEGORY	UNSATISFACTORY	MARGINAL
JOB SPECIFICS	**JOB KNOWLEDGE**	Unsatisfactory job knowledge, shows little interest in improving.	Needs improvement. Requires coaching & instructions.
	QUALITY OF WORK	Consistently low in accuracy, work must always be checked.	Accuracy is often inconsistent. Work must be checked.
	MAINTENANCE OF BUILDING	Often fails to address maintenance and repair issues on a timely basis—creates additional cost for the building	Occasionally fails to address maintenance and repair issues on a timely basis—creates additional cost for the building.
MANAGEMENT SKILLS	**JUDGMENT & DECISION MAKING ABILITY**	Indecisive or makes snap decisions without a factual basis. Often comes to wrong conclusions.	Often fails to give proper regard to facts or tends to procrastinate. Decisions are not consistent/reliable.
	SUPERVISORY ABILITY	Provides inadequate information and direction to subordinates.	Some supervisory skills that need improvement.
	COOPERATION/COURTESY TO CO-WORKERS AND RESIDENTS	Frequently causes or contributes to unrest or friction with co-workers and residents.	Occasionally abrasive. Seldom offers to help co-workers and residents.
	COST MANAGEMENT	Often does not manage building expenditures on a cost-effective basis.	Occasionally manages building expenditures on a cost-effective basis.
	COMMUNICATION WITH BOARD AND RESIDENTS	Has difficulty in expressing simple ideas or information clearly.	Occasionally has difficulty in making effective presentations.
GENERAL	**RESPONSIVENESS**	Output below average. Fails to complete tasks within acceptable time limits.	Must be pushed to complete tasks within time limits.
	HEALTH & SAFETY AWARENESS	No knowledge of Health & Safety at Work.	Some recollection of the existence of Health & Safety.
	MANNER & SELF ASSURANCE	Often seems unsure of self, does not handle stressful situations well.	Needs to improve, often loses composure under stress.

Reviewer:

COMPETENT	COMMENDABLE	OUTSTANDING
Good level of knowledge of own job. Adapts well to changing conditions.	Thorough understanding of own job and good level of knowledge in related areas.	Recognized as an authority in own area and related areas.
Work meets an acceptable standard of accuracy.	High quality work. Mistakes seldom occur.	Consistently accurate and thorough in all job assignments.
Maintains the building and addresses repairs as they arise.	Has good foresight and generally practices preventive maintenance and repairs of building.	Is proactive about preventive maintenance and repairs of building.
Make fairly prompt and firm decisions. Gives consideration to relevant facts.	Obtains facts and applies sound reasoning. Takes prompt action.	Conducts thorough analysis of all facts, makes definite decisions with consistent promptness. Excellent decision maker.
Demonstrates good supervisory skills, gets results.	Gets excellent results with minimum of personnel problems	Obtains trust, respect & outstanding results from people.
Gets along well in work relationship with co-workers and residents.	Highly co-operative, offers to assist co-workers and residents whenever possible.	Exceptional in giving & obtaining co-operation with co-workers and residents.
Good management of building expenditures and adheres to cost savings practices.	Usually applies good planning for purchases and employs cost savings techniques on behalf of building.	Excellent planning for purchases and always employs cost savings techniques on behalf of the building.
Expresses ideas and information in clear and concise manner in most situations.	Very effective in communicating ideas and information.	Exceptionally skillful in communicating complex ideas & information.
Meets most standards on assigned tasks. Satisfactory amount completed within time scale.	Completes tasks promptly. Excellent use of work time.	Exceptionally fast and efficient in all duties and assignments.
Practices good Health & Safety.	Occasionally has input to Health and Safety issues.	Has regular input to the Board of Managers on Health and Safety issues.
Makes a good impression and gains respect. Usually remains calm under stress.	Makes an excellent impression in work relationships. Very good tolerance for stress.	Makes an outstanding impression in work relationships, complete self control under stress.

continued

SUPERINTENDENT PERFORMANCE EVALUATION continued

CATEGORY	UNSATISFACTORY	MARGINAL

COMMENTS / ISSUES

SCORING GRID

- **A tick in the:**

Unsatisfactory	scores 1
Marginal	scores 2
Competent	scores 3
Commendable	scores 4
Outstanding	scores 5

Signature Superintendent: _____

PRINT NAME: _____

DATE: _____

COMPETENT	COMMENDABLE	OUTSTANDING

- **Categories:**

    There are a total of 11 categories.

    To achieve final score the total of the ticked boxes is divided by 11 or however many categories have been scored.

    (a) TOTAL OF SCORES IN BOXES

    (b) NO. OF CATEGORIES SCORED

    (c) AVERAGE FINAL SCORE [(a)/(b)]

Signature Board Member _____

PRINT NAME: _____

DATE: _____

CHAPTER 7

LONG-TERM PLANNING:

Maintenance, Budget and Insurance

Accurate long-term planning is crucial in maintaining the integrity of all the operations, facilities and financial aspects of your property. While this might be your home, it must be managed as a business. Long-term plans must be prepared and updated on an annual basis. The service of analyzing, preparing and implementing a Long-Term Plan most definitely falls under the responsibility of your property manager. Most management companies have a team in place to effectuate such plans. These teams are usually composed of the Chief Financial Officer, Vice President of Operations (or similar personnel responsible for implementing and overseeing operational issues company-wide) and your assigned property manager.

Operational Long-Term Planning
Staffing: All aspects of staffing must be reviewed as a crucial part of any Long-Term Plan, including the following questions. What staffing issues might we be dealing with in the near future? Must we begin a search for new employees due to upcoming retirements? How will future capital work affect the staffing of the property? Will the renovated hallways require more or less maintenance? By automating the elevators will we be able to reduce staff? Will these

be Union personnel? If so, what are the requirements to implement the reduction of staff?

Supplies and Services: I am sure many of you are surprised to see supplies and services listed as a topic under Operational Long-Term Planning. But, believe it or not, a little foresight in this area can save you substantial funds in the future. For example, almost every property out there utilizes large quantities of plastic trash bags. Properties with compactors can go through several hundred cases in a year. Do you realize that the plastic used to produce these bags is an oil-based material? Therefore, during cold winters, when the price of oil usually increases, so does the price of all items made from oil-based materials, such as plastic bags. Therefore, we recommend that these products be purchased and inventoried during the summer months. The same concept holds true with regard to many service providers. For instance, many large cities now have ordinances in place requiring cyclical inspections of building facades followed up by performing required repairs. If you are aware that work must be done on your property, you will get a much better price doing it on an off year, rather than a year in which a governmental agency is requiring inspections and work be performed on all properties. The reason is simple; the less work out there, the more competitive the bidding is by service providers for the jobs.

Other areas to look into are how world events affect your operating expenses. For example, if you foresee rising fuel prices, what can be done to prepare for these increased costs? Possibly install a new, more effective heat timer on the boiler or a more effective pool heater. Both of these actions will curtail usage, thereby reducing expenditures. What are the increased costs associated with next year's union employee contract (if your property is unionized)? How can they be offset? Can you curtail overtime?

Another important area in which long-term planning can result in substantial savings for your property is fuel buying. Locking-in fuel prices by contracting with a supplier before the heat season begins will allow your property to get the best possible price, whether you are buying oil or natural gas. Most companies offer a price guarantee as long as you pay up front by the end of September. While this does entail committing a large sum of money all at once, if the cost of fuel rises during the winter, as it often does, you will still receive the pre-heat-season price. In most cases, if the cost of fuel drops, you will be credited for any over-payment, so there is nothing to lose.

Fuel buying groups can also help your property get a discount on oil and gas. By joining groups such as the New York Public Interest Research Group (NYPIRG), consumers can save a substantial amount on their fuel bills. For a low annual fee, NYPIRG members can save 25 cents or more per gallon. Multiplied by the large quantity of fuel that most buildings use, especially in cold northern climates, that can add up to real savings.

Insurance: Don't ever underestimate the importance of insurance in your property's long-term planning. Whether you are protecting your property from one of Florida's hurricanes or your board members from one of New York's infamous liability lawsuits, your property must be sure to have adequate insurance coverage. Your managing company should have a number of trusted insurance companies that they work with regularly, but be sure to get proposals from several firms and be sure to compare apples to apples when looking at different policies.

Even if you believe that your insurance policies are all in place and have been chosen properly, it's important to have them reevaluated periodically. Property inspections can often result in considerable premium reductions, while an appraisal can ensure that your board is not paying for more insurance that it needs. One Manhattan co-op discovered that it was overinsured by about $15,000,000 and correcting the problem led to a reduction in each unit owner's insurance bill of about $600 a year. On the other hand, underinsuring your property can be even more costly. When it comes to liability insurance, be sure to consult an attorney as well as your manager and insurance agent. Directors & Officers

Insurance protects board members from liability in the decision-making they do for the property. An overall umbrella policy may be an inexpensive way to increase your property's liability coverage without unduly increasing premiums.

In addition to regular review of your policies and periodic audits and appraisals, there are other methods of keeping insurance costs in check. Security features such as alarms, video monitors, smoke detectors and carbon monoxide detectors can all help reduce premiums, as can upgraded electrical and plumbing systems, roof repairs, and installation of sprinklers. In addition, boards should require unit owners to carry individual apartment owners' insurance so that the building does not get embroiled in claims that should rightfully be covered by the resident's insurance.

Compliance: Keeping up with current legal requirements of co-ops, condos and homeowners' associations is a job in itself. Board members must rely on their professionals to keep them abreast of ever-changing regulations in the areas of taxation, property maintenance, recycling, and safety issues. Filing paperwork on time and complying with the laws are vital to your property's health. Not only will you avoid costly fines and penalties, but you will protect your fellow residents from lawsuits.

Capital Long-Term Planning
Capital Plans are a key element in assuring that your property runs effectively and efficiently for years to come. While the plan is clearly only an estimate, it is the only way you can responsibly identify your future financial requirements. Due to the fact that these plans are estimates, it is imperative that they be reviewed and updated on an annual basis.

The major components of the Capital Plan submitted to you by your manager should consist of the following sections:

Capital Components List: A comprehensive list must be compiled of all potential capital requirements on site. This includes roofs, elevators, mechanical equipment, fitness equipment, heating/ cooling plants and cosmetics such as hallways and party rooms.

Remaining Useful Life: Each physical component of your property has a useful life associated with it. For example, most roofing systems have anywhere from a ten to 15-year life expectancy (this varies tremendously in different parts of the country due to the variables of climate and elements). If you installed your system three years ago and it had a life expectancy of ten years, you currently have a remaining life expectancy of seven years. In other areas, you must be more subjective. For instance, identifying how much longer you have before you will be required to refurbish your party room is something that must be carefully looked at and discussed. You must analyze the current condition, take into account how the room is used, and come up with an estimate.

Future Dollar Costing: It is now time to take the above items and come up with projected replacement costs upon the termination of their projected useful life. This is not as difficult as it seems. Most management companies should have enough historical data on hand to perform this task. Vendors and service providers can often be very helpful in this area.

Financial Long-Term Planning
Funding: Now that we have completed our Capital Plan, we can calculate what our future capital funding requirements will be. Once this is determined, various suggestions should be presented by your management team as to how to meet your funding requirements. These recommendations could be as basic as an assessment, increased common charges to build reserves, or some sort of financing. It is important to have all alternatives explored and presented to you in depth prior to your choosing one. Depending on whether you are a condominium, Homeowners Association, cooperative or cond-op, the different methods of raising the funds could have varying tax implications on both the overall entity or the individual owners.

Future Cost Increases: There are numerous day-to-day operating expenses, which we know will increase drastically over time, that can be addressed in advance to lessen the burden on owners. Even if nothing can be done to reduce these expenditures, just notifying your owners in advance will assist them in meeting their obligations. An example of such increases in cost would be the loss of a tax abatement. Often, when new properties are developed or existing ones are upgraded, the local and/or federal government grants a tax abatement for several years. Upon the termination of such abatements, owners will realize huge increases in their tax liabilities. This is something that your owners should be consistently reminded of in advance. In addition, if you are aware that the costs associated with your staff will increase dramatically in three years due to a contractual obligation, perhaps you can phase in the increase to your owners over time.

On-Going Capital Improvements

Whether you are upgrading your elevators, installing a new boiler, surfacing roadways, redecorating the lobby or waterproofing the facade, chances are your property is nearly always overseeing or planning a capital improvement project. With big jobs come big bills, and the opportunity for problems to arise. Working with a management company that can take full responsibility for overseeing your on-going capital improvement projects will take a big load off your mind.

From the beginning stages of planning, through the final stages of sign-off, a professional Project Manager will see to it that every aspect of the job is done correctly. You should expect your manager to provide on-site inspections, coordinate scheduling, and review performance and warranties.

Don't run the risk of hiring an overpriced or under-experienced contractor, or one whose finances are not 100 percent reliable. Situations such as these can lead to incomplete or unsatisfactory jobs, leaving the board and residents to foot the bill to correct the problem. In one Upper East Side cooperative, a major lobby renovation was begun only to unravel as the contractor faced financial difficulties. After a year of work, the lobby currently sits unfinished, with construction debris decorating the entrance of this prime location. Such a renovation disaster can have calamitous repercussions for residents trying to sell their units, not to mention the inconvenience of having to walk through an unfinished lobby every day. One midtown Manhattan condo hired a contractor to repave the sidewalk in front of the building's entrance. The beautiful grey granite paving stones were laid and looked perfect at first. As it turned out, however, the engineer had provided the wrong specifications. Within weeks the stones had begun to crack and the entire job had to be ripped up and reinstalled. The result was a huge inconvenience to residents, as well as an enormous expense to the condo.

The answer? Never begin a major capital project without consulting the professionals first and without working with a Project Manager who can oversee the entire job. If the work is structural in nature, you must enlist the professional assistance of an engineer or architect who will analyze the problem and propose a solution, write the specifications, and ensure that the contractor's work is up to par. In addition, all contracts should be looked over by an attorney well-versed in this area. The bids and the work of each professional should be cleared through one overseeing professional to protect you from unfinished or below par workmanship.

What it all boils down to is the fact that no organization can run well without always keeping an eye on the future. While it might be well and good that your property manager handles your day-to-day operations superbly, if he does not perform long-term planning for you, he is doing you and your community a tremendous disservice.

CHAPTER 8

CONCLUSION

Your home is probably the biggest single investment you will ever make, and perhaps your greatest financial asset. As such, it's important to protect and maximize its long-term value. And because a home is so much more than an investment, it's equally important to ensure the quality of life that it affords you as owner and resident. Living in a multi-housing property means working together with your fellow residents to meet your shared goals, which can be both challenging and rewarding.

Board members have the responsibility of setting the tone of leadership for the property, as well as hiring and overseeing the professional manager. As with any volunteer board, whether they are running a not-for-profit foundation or a housing facility, the key to success is to create workable systems, clear delineation of responsibility and open lines of communication. Boards must set policy for the property from a position of knowledge, and then leave the implementation of that policy to their professional management company. Knowing what to expect from your managing agent on a daily, weekly, monthly and annual basis will allow the board to monitor the progress and effectiveness of the management firm they have chosen.

It's imperative that boards act quickly when systems are not followed or expectations are not met. The best way to solve such problems quickly is by speaking directly with your manager, or if more help is needed, the manager's supervisor or the company's principals. The importance of good communication in both routine situations and unusual ones cannot be overemphasized. Don't settle for less than you expect. As a homeowner you deserve the service you have been promised, and your professional manager has pledged to provide you that service in the form of your management contract.

A board that focuses on the common good of the property, working together with a committed, professional management firm, has the power to protect both the investment value and the quality of life for every one of its residents. It's a goal that cannot be taken lightly, and one that is often frustrating, time-consuming and difficult. Nevertheless, with the right guidance, such a board can keep its property looking great, running smoothly and operating efficiently for many years to come.

RESOURCES

In New York:

New York City Department of Housing Preservation and Development
Description of laws and related information and Housing Education Program
phone: 311 in NYC or (212) NEW YORK
website: www.nyc.gov/html/hpd

New York City Department of Environment Protection
Information on lead hazards, remediation and training
phone: (800) 424-LEAD (5323)
website: www.epa.gov/lead

New York City Department of Finance
Real property information
Dial 311 in NYC or (212) NEW YORK
website: www.nyc.gov/html/dof

Service Employees International Union (SEIU) Local 32BJ
President: Mike Fishman
(212) 388-3500
website: www.seiu32bj.org

New York City Department of Finance
Real Estate Tax Abatement Program information
website: www.nyc.gov/html/dof/html/exemptions.html

New York City Department of Buildings
Codes, forms, filing, etc.
(212) 566-5000
website: www.nyc.gov/html/dob/home.html

The Official Directory of Co-op & Condo Services
Published by Yale Robbins Publications, LLC.
(212) 683-5700
www.yrpubs.com

New York Association of Realty Managers (NYARM)
(212) 216-0654
www.nyarm.org

Superintendents Technical Association
(718) 552-1161
www.nysupersclub.org

New York Building Managers Association
(212) 755-2159
www.nybma.org

The Cooperator
Monthly publication, annual Co-op & Condo Expo
212) 683-5700
website: cooperator.com

Council of NY Cooperatives & Condominiums
Membership organization, annual educational conference
(212) 496-7400
website: cnyc.com

Federation of NY Housing Cooperatives & Condominiums
Membership organization, annual conference
(718) 760-7540
website: fnyhc.coop

Insurance Information Institute
(212) 346-500
website: iii.org

New York State Energy Research & Development Authority (NYSERDA)
(212) 971-5342
website: nyserda.org

In Florida:

Florida Senate
Legislation, etc.
website: flsenate.gov

Florida House of Representatives
Legislation, etc.
website: myfloridahouse.gov

Florida Department of Business and Professional Regulation
Homeowners' Association Task Force
website: myflorida.com/dbpr

State of Florida
Legislative and real estate information
website: stateofflorida.com

About My HOA
Communication site for neighborhoods, HOAs, and communities
website: aboutmyhoa.com

Community Associations Institute
Non-profit alliance serving community associations
phone: 888-CAI-4321
website: caionline.org

Florida Homeowners Associated
Providing information and links to Florida homeowners' needs
website: florida-homeowners.com

U.S. Department of Housing and Urban Development
Ownership, financing and emergency information
Miami phone: (305) 536-4456 Fax (305) 536-5765
website: hud.gov

ABOUT THE AUTHOR

Leslie Kaminoff
Chief Executive Officer, Akam Living Services, Inc.

As founder and CEO of Akam Living Services, Inc., Leslie Kaminoff has earned a reputation for honesty, integrity and experience. He frequently shares his expertise with the owners, boards and professionals of cooperatives, condominiums and Homeowners Associations through articles, lectures and teaching engagements. He is co-author of the book, "How to Choose the Right Management Company for Your Residential Property."

Founded by Mr. Kaminoff, Akam Living Services is the parent company of Akam Associates in Manhattan, Akam South in Boca Raton, Florida, Akam Sales & Brokerage, and The Complete Concierge. The Akam group manages and provides sales and homeowners support services to its client properties in the New York Metropolitan area and in South Florida. Now in its 20th year of operation, Akam maintains offices in both locations, with over 125 professional managers and support staff.

Mr. Kaminoff is a member of numerous professional organizations, including the Associated Builders and Owners of Greater New York, the Community Associations Institute, the Real Estate Board of New York and the New York Association of Realty Managers, where he has served as Director. He is a past Governor of the New York Chapter of Registered Apartment Managers, and has won numerous awards for excellence in management from publications such as *Habitat* and *The Cooperator*, as well as industry organizations.

Leslie Kaminoff splits his time between Akam's offices in Midtown Manhattan and their offices in Boca Raton, Florida, and is a homeowner in both locations. When not in Manhattan, he spends his time with his wife and two children in Palm Beach County.

ORDER FORM

For additional copies of *What to Expect from Your Property Manager*, please fill out the form below and mail it to:

Akam Living Services, Inc.
6421 Congress Avenue, Suite 110
Boca Raton, FL 33487
(561) 994-4870

or visit our website at akam.com

Name: _____

Address: _____

_____

Phone: _____

Email address: _____

My building is a ❑ Co-op ❑ Condo ❑ HOA

I am a ❑ Board Member ❑ Unit owner ❑ Manager
❑ Other Real Estate Professional

Number of copies: _____ Cost per copy is $19.95

Amount enclosed: $_____

❑ Check enclosed (payable to Akam)

❑ Charge to my credit card

❑ American Express ❑ Visa ❑ Master Card

Name on card: _____

Account number _____ Expiration Date: _____

Mailing Address (if different from above):

_____

_____

_____

Printed in Canada